PROOF OF HEAVEN?

A MENTAL ILLUSIONIST EXAMINES THE AFTERLIFE EXPERIENCE OF EBEN ALEXANDER, M.D. FROM A BIBLICAL VIEWPOINT

by

Coleman Luck

The Sandstar Group

The Sandstar Group
POB 3613
Oakhurst, CA 93644
www.colemanluck.com

Quotes are from: Proof of Heaven: A Neurosurgeon's Journey Into the Afterlife
by Eben Alexander, M.D., Simon and Shuster Paperbacks. © 2012 Eben
Alexander, M.D.

Scripture taken from the New King James Version®. Copyright © 1982 by
Thomas Nelson, Inc. Used by permission. All rights reserved.

To the good memory of the many people who taught me about God, especially those who hurt me and, thereby, helped God prepare a stubborn soul for Heaven.

"Your soul has a curious shape because it is a hollow made to fit a particular swelling in the infinite contours of the divine substance, or a key to unlock one of the doors in the house with many mansions. For it is not humanity in the abstract that is to be saved, but you – you the individual reader...Blessed and fortunate creature, your eyes shall behold Him and not another's. All that you are, sins apart, is destined, if you will let God have His good way, to utter satisfaction...Your place in Heaven will seem to be made for you and you alone, because you were made for it."

C.S. Lewis
The Problem of Pain

Table of Contents:

1. Who Am I?
2. Who or what will guide your life?
3. What if a doctor came back from the dead?
4. Is this a proof of Heaven?
5. The first questions:
6. Escaping the "womb" of death.
7. Welcome to the Core.
8. The message from "Om".
9. Can we be separated from God?
10. What did Dr. Alexander really experience?
11. What questions should he have asked?
12. Which will you believe?

Chapter One

Who am I?

I am a mentalist and a member of the Academy of Magical Arts at the world-famous Magic Castle in Hollywood. Beginning in my teenage years (I am now 67), I have spent a significant portion of my life studying illusions and our deep susceptibility to them. As a performer, I know how easy it is for the most intelligent and sophisticated among us to be utterly befuddled by the simplest forms of trickery.

For a number of years I have been presenting an evening of mental illusions called "Illusions of Power." In this program I perform many effects that appear to be psychic or supernatural in origin, including mindreading, predictions, psychokinesis, spirit contact and much more.

For half the program, I present these effects as though I had real power. But at a certain point, I stop and inform the audience that everything they have seen has been an illusion. I have no psychic or supernatural abilities. Though I never tell how I perform illusions, I make it very clear that everything they have seen has been caused by subtle trickery. Then, I talk about why we are so easily fooled.

Over and over I have observed a disturbing phenomenon. Even after being as clear as possible that everything they have seen has been a trick, there are audience members who refuse to believe me.

After one program a young woman came forward and said to me, "When you told me that you were entering my mind, I could just feel it. It was so strange." I informed her that, whatever she had felt, it had nothing to do with my entering her mind. I had never done such a thing. What she had experienced had been generated entirely inside her own head because she believed what I had told her. I had a difficult time convincing her of that and she is far from the only one.

Why are humans so easily influenced? Because most of us desperately want to believe that there is more to life than what we see, that strange hidden powers are possible and there are people who have them. When we lose loved ones, in our sorrow and loneliness, we long to communicate with them. We want to know where they are. Do their spirits continue on? Do they still love and remember us?

After one program, a very sophisticated gentleman who had been a top-level executive in an international corporation came up to me. Several years before, he had lost his wife. With tears in his eyes he asked whether it might be possible to communicate with her. I told him what I believe very strongly after years of research, that, no, it is not possible. When you go to a medium, you are not communicating with the one you lost, no matter how much it might appear that way.

I am not only a mentalist. For many years, I was a professional writer and executive producer of television in Hollywood, the heart of illusion in the world today. During my career (I am a Life Member of the Writers Guild of America, West) I was privileged to be a television series showrunner and series creator.

As a professional storyteller I have come to believe one thing with absolute certainty, story controls the world. Individually, stories define our relationships, our political attitudes, our views of what is real and what isn't. Collectively, stories define and control entire cultures. As a people's belief in stories changes, cultures change either for better or worse. Stories can either build us up or tear us down, and both kinds can be very enticing.

Chapter Two

Who or what will guide your life?

The crisis issue of our time is the issue of authority. What authority will each of us choose to guide our lives? For most people today the answer is, "I'm my own authority. I choose to believe and do whatever I want. I will decide what is true and what isn't, what is good for me and what is not." But, very often, this doesn't work well, because we humans are so easily influenced, manipulated and fooled.

Jesus said that people are like sheep without a shepherd. He was right. We want to make our own choices and run our own lives, but there is something inside all of us that desperately desires a king or a president or a father or a mother or a mentor to guide us.

Our desire for someone knowledgeable and strong whom we can trust when we are in trouble was the basis for the 1980's TV series I am best known for called The Equalizer. It starred a wonderful British actor named Edward Woodward. He played Robert McCall, the ultimate father figure. When you were in desperate trouble with nowhere to turn he would be there.

Several years ago a woman wrote to me from Australia. She said that when she was a child she would watch The Equalizer every week. Her home life was so bad that it was the only thing that gave her hope. Our series showed her what a father would be like. In this case, a story was a positive influence.

Unfortunately, this need to trust someone whom we think is intelligent, ethical, reliable and, perhaps, powerful, is the cause of many mistakes in human life, both individually and collectively. Too often the people we trust prove to be unreliable. Perhaps their intentions were good, they just weren't able to perform. And then there are those few whose intentions aren't good.

Complicating the situation, our culture manipulates us to trust certain authority figures above others. For instance, we have been trained to think that science has the answer or eventually will find the answer to almost every human dilemma. After all, isn't it science that has brought us so much comfort and wealth?

We have been trained to place our faith in scientists believing that they have the intellect, education and objectivity to discover and understand what is true and what isn't. This is one of the great myths of our culture.

We don't consider that most scientists operate in significantly constrained environments controlled by academia and government. We don't consider that so many live under the iron fist of stringent and often nonsensical political requirements unique to their disciplines. We don't consider that the Law of Unintended Consequences has brought almost as much disaster on the human race through scientific discoveries as it has brought blessings. We don't consider that scientists are people just like us who make mistakes and serious errors of judgment both in their work and their personal lives.

Of all scientists, physicians have our greatest respect and trust. We pride ourselves on making our own choices, yet when a health crisis arises we quickly place our lives into their hands. We believe doctors to be (and most often are) ethical people concerned for our welfare. Companies marketing products understand this level of trust. That's why they use doctors, or actors playing doctors, to sell us their products.

Physicians hold such an important place because the truth is that we all have a terminal disease. That disease is called life. From the moment we are born we begin to die. When we become old enough to realize that death is waiting, a great shadow starts looming over us. When we lose friends and loved ones the shadow grows much larger. Whether we admit it or not, death and what, if anything, comes afterward is the ultimate concern of the human race.

Chapter Three

What if a doctor came back from the dead?

What if there was a scientist, a brilliant, supremely ethical individual trained in observation, who experienced what happens after death, then came back and reported what he saw? And what if he wasn't just a scientist, he was a medical scientist and a doctor, a man of compassion. Wouldn't that be amazing? If someone like that appeared wouldn't you be strongly inclined to believe what he said? After all, such a person would never lie and how could he ever be fooled?

As I said, I am a mentalist. Sadly, in the long history of mentalism and fraudulent psychic phenomena, some of the people most easily fooled have been scientists. Why has this been so? Perhaps there are two reasons: Some tend to be arrogant. With arrogance, they assume that they are so intelligent and their systems are so well designed that no one could outsmart them.

The second reason may be surprising. Many are naïve. They are naïve because, as secular humanists, they don't understand or even believe in the true nature of evil. If they have any practical concept of evil at all, it is the simplistic perspective of popular culture and personal experience. And why should it not be otherwise? After all, they aren't philosophers, they are scientists.

When he began his practice, noted psychiatrist M. Scott Peck discovered that he was unprepared to handle a certain group of people who came to him for psychotherapy. They didn't fit into any category that he had been trained to handle, so he had to create a new one. That category was "Evil." Dr. Peck discovered that real evil existed in some of the people who came to him, but often it was well camouflaged. From these therapeutic experiences he wrote a book entitled <u>The People of the Lie</u>.

Understanding evil is not an easy or comfortable thing to attempt. It can be frightening especially when we realize that some of the worst evil can appear to be ravishingly beautiful, joyful, comforting, even filled with ecstasy. Deadly traps are never set with flashing signs that warn, DON'T WALK HERE OR YOU WILL DIE. They're baited with desire. They can be baited with stunning loveliness.

The naivete of scientists is well documented. Mentalists and fake psychics learned a long time ago that, in too many cases, once a scientist trusts you and becomes a friend, you can get away with almost anything. If you doubt this, I suggest you do some research. Begin with the name Steve Shaw, who performs as a mentalist under the name Banachek and has worked with a magician researcher named James Randi, who is known as The Amazing Randi.

In 1979 then chairman of McDonnell-Douglas Aircraft, James S. McDonnell, announced an unusual grant. Because of his

long interest in the paranormal he had
donated $500,000 to Washington University
in St. Louis to create what became known as
the McDonnell Laboratory for Psychical
Research.

The director, Peter R. Phillips, a
scientist who had spent a decade studying
parapsychology, announced to the press that
the center would focus on psychokinetic
metal bending among children. James Randi
viewed this as an opportunity to prove that
such "research" was seriously biased due to a
lack of objectivity and shoddy protocols. He
believed that the intelligent and trained
scientists who would be running the tests
could be easily fooled by simple, but well-
executed illusions.

To prove this, he enlisted the help of
two teenage mentalists who volunteered to
participate in the program. Of course, their
true backgrounds were not known to the
researchers. One of them was Steve Shaw.

Even as his two secret volunteers
entered the program, James Randi offered his
services to the scientists as an expert in
fraudulent phenomena to help discover

anyone who might try to fool them. His offer was ignored.

Over the next four years, including 160 hours of laboratory testing, a whole range of ill-conceived experiments were conducted with the two young mentalists. Over and over, they seemed to prove the existence of real psychic power. The duped scientists were exultant. In reality what had they seen? Nothing but trickery from the start.

As had been planned from the beginning, finally the truth was revealed. What was the only *fact* that had been proven in this long and expensive project? Because they were arrogant and naïve, scientists who claimed to be skilled, knowledgeable and sophisticated researchers could be easily fooled by well-constructed illusions. It was very embarrassing.

As a mentalist who knows the craft of illusion I come to any discussion of the supernatural or paranormal with a healthy dose of skepticism. However, I am not a materialist skeptic. I have seen too much in my 67 years to believe that what can be experienced with the five senses and replicated using the scientific method is the limit of reality. We live in a mysterious world filled with strange anomalies.

Also, I am a Christian. When I say that, it means that I have accepted an ultimate authority to guide my life that is outside myself. That authority is the Bible. For me, there is good and sufficient evidence that the Bible is what it claims to be, the supernatural message from the Eternal God and Creator about ultimate reality. That message is for every person on earth and I can tell you that, long ago, it transformed my life.

As a Christian, the Bible is my measuring stick to test every truth- claim regarding ultimate reality. Issues of ultimate reality include the meaning and purpose of life, what happens after death in eternity, and how we can have a relationship with God. After all the years, I can say that the Bible has never failed me. We're going to use it now.

Chapter Four

Is this a proof of Heaven?

Last year a book was published that has brought a great deal of media attention because it claims to be an authoritative statement about the afterlife as personally witnessed by a brilliant, apparently unimpeachable, and highly ethical, trained observer. The book is entitled: Proof of Heaven: A Scientist's Case for the Afterlife and was written by Dr. Eben Alexander, an academic neurosurgeon who has practiced and taught at Harvard Medical School and other institutions.

In <u>Proof of Heaven,</u> Dr. Alexander states that he considered himself to be a Christian long before the crisis recorded in his book. However, it's clear from his own admission that he was a Christian in name only, who rarely attended church and, one must assume, rarely read the Bible. As he admits, he was a secular materialist who had little faith in anything that couldn't be proven with the five senses under the control of an educated and disciplined mind. During his years of practice, he had heard many near death experiences from patients, but had never taken any of them seriously, believing them to be caused by nothing more than chemical changes in the brain.

On November 10, 2008, Dr. Alexander awoke to throbbing pain at the base of his spine. Very quickly, it grew much worse. He didn't know it, but he had contracted bacterial meningitis. The specific form was E. Coli which is extremely rare in adults.

With tremendous speed, the infection attacked his cerebral cortex causing it to completely stop functioning. That is one definition of death. Dr. Alexander was brain dead for days. Specialists, some of whom were his own colleagues, finally told his family that there was no hope. They should pull the plug and acknowledge that he was gone.

The experiences that Dr. Alexander had, what he witnessed, during those days when he was brain dead, are the main subject of his book and this study.

At the very start I want to say that there are Christians who call Dr. Alexander a liar because of what he reports. They think that he can't have seen what he claims, so he must be fabricating the entire thing. In my opinion, such people are both insulting and wrong.

It is clear to me that Dr. Alexander is a man of high ethical values. By writing this book he took a deep risk within his own scientific community and has faced rejection because of it. I believe that Dr. Alexander saw and experienced exactly what he describes and much more. It was totally real to him. He is telling the absolute truth about what happened to him as he understands it.

At the other extreme are Christians who accept Dr. Alexander's report at face value, thinking that what he has written confirms their hope and faith. In my opinion, they are just as wrong.

Perhaps most foolish of all are those who view <u>Proof of Heaven</u> as a rather whimsical and unimportant work that needn't be taken seriously, just one of many books written from "the fringe."

The record of Dr. Alexander's experience is extremely important on several levels which we are going to examine. We will measure some of his central experiences and truth claims regarding God and the afterlife against the witness of the Bible. It will be up to each reader to determine which of those witnesses to believe because they do not agree.

I will be quoting and synopsizing from <u>Proof of Heaven</u>, but I strongly recommend that the reader purchase the book. It is well written and filled with many details that cannot be discussed here, including the record of the medical procedures and events involved in this unusual case.

For seven days, Dr. Alexander was not conscious of anything in this world. But according to his statements, what he was experiencing during that time was far more real than anything that he had ever experienced to that point in his entire life. Here is what happened:

After becoming unconscious, Dr. Alexander awoke to what he called "visible darkness." (page 29) In his words it was like being submerged in "mud or dirty Jell-o." This darkness was claustrophobic and suffocating. He describes it as a kind of vast muddy womb. Eventually there came from somewhere a deep, pounding, mechanical roar like a giant subterranean blacksmith striking an anvil. The sound reverberated everywhere.

I have read many, many near death experiences. Never have I read one that began in such a way. In particular, one reality that he faced is most unusual. From the moment of his awakening in this very strange and disturbing environment, Dr. Alexander was not aware that he had any kind of body.

In fact, he had no personality. Throughout the entire experience, from beginning to end, he states that he did not know who he was or even that he was an independent being. As he describes it, language, emotion and logic all were gone as though he had entered some kind of "primordial state."

The visible darkness where he found himself became increasingly uncomfortable. He says that it felt like being a mole or an earthworm. At some point, up out of the mud-like ooze rose grotesque animal faces that "groaned and screeched," and became "increasingly threatening." Dr. Alexander began to feel unseen creatures slithering past. The unpleasant environment was made much worse by the odor of feces or vomit. To him, it was the smell of biological death.

According to Dr. Alexander, he was in this uncomfortable and disturbing place for an indefinite period. "days? Months? Years?" There was no way of knowing. As his existence went on, he began to feel that he didn't belong there and had to get out. He started to experience panic. Later he called this the realm of the earthworm's-eye view and sank back into it repeatedly during the course of the vision.

Chapter Five

The first questions:

Here, at the very start of Dr. Alexander's afterlife adventure, we confront some important issues. The first is his total loss of personhood – no memory, no sense of personal history, no individual existence, not even the awareness of a physical body, though, clearly, he could feel, see and smell what was going on around him. In his later analysis, during his time in the afterlife he considered himself not a man, not an animal, not really anything at all.

We must ask, why was he placed in this state for the duration of the experience?

Could it have been necessary that his logical mind be stripped away so that he would be more susceptible to what he was being shown?

Dr. Alexander reports that as he began to experience the lovely vision of heaven, periodically, he was re-immersed into the disgusting and frightening environment of the "Earthworm's-Eye View?" Why did this happen? We cannot help but ask whether it might have served to keep him pliable and more appreciative of "heaven" each time the vision returned?

Such repeated psychological dislocation is consistent with techniques of brainwashing. The purpose of such techniques is, first, to destroy individuality through fear and isolation. After that, through a system of powerful negative and positive experiences, the victim is reduced to a childlike state where he willingly accepts whatever truth-claim is presented to him. Whether we accept the brainwashing analogy or not, in Dr. Alexander's case, the end result was the same.

If what he was being shown really was Heaven, why not let the man enjoy it with every resource of his humanity including his trained, logical mind intact. Why re-immerse him in ugliness?

However, as a Christian, to me the most important question of all is, does this loss of personhood at death and entry into Heaven through ugliness square with anything in the Bible?

In **John 14:1** Jesus says this to His disciples: **"Let not your heart be troubled; you believe in God, believe also in Me. In My Father's house are many mansions; if it were not so, I would have told you. I go to prepare a place for you. And if I go and prepare a place for you, I will come again and receive you to Myself; that where I am, there you may be also.** (All Biblical quotes are from the New King James Version.)

And a short time later He said to them in **John 14:27**: **"Peace I leave with you, My peace I give to you; not as the world gives do I give to you. Let not your heart be troubled, neither let it be afraid."**

Those words were meant for all believers in Jesus. The Gospel of John was written to non-Jewish readers. For people who lived in the ancient pagan world, death was a terrifying mystery.

To the Greeks, the afterlife was a place of dark shadows where the newly dead would confront a river called Styx, a word that means hate and detestation. A ghostly boat would arrive to take them across to the land of the dead, a world of gloom and darkness where the individual would become a bodiless ghost or "shade."

If you were Egyptian, you believed that at death you would stand before the dog-faced god Anubis who would weigh your heart against a feather to see if you were worthy to progress upward.

What Jesus said to His followers flew in the face of thousands of years of pagan religion. He was saying, "I am going away to where God, my Father, is and in that vast domain I'm going to build a place for you to live. That place will be your new home after death. That home is my home. I'll be there with you."

Clearly, this implies several things. First, it implies the peace and comfort of going home. And all of us have experienced that, haven't we? Certainly, Jesus is communicating that there will be no discomfort, no ugliness and no terror in the home that he was preparing for His followers. No -Earthworm's-Eye View.

Second, and basic to all of this, is the powerful implication that at death there will be no loss of personhood. Can you imagine Jesus saying, "I'm going to prepare a place for you, but when you get there you won't have a clue who you are. You won't have any memory. You won't even know that you're a person. But don't be afraid. And, by the way, when you first get there it will seem like you're drowning in a squishy hell-like womb for a few years. Not to worry."

Notice that Jesus uses the familiar personal pronouns, "I" and "you." How can this mean anything less than that He will know us and we will know Him. If that is the case, certainly, we will know ourselves.

In **2 Corinthians 5:1-8**, the Apostle Paul writes this: **For we know that if our earthly house, this tent, is destroyed, we have a building from God, a house not made with hands, eternal in the heavens. 2 For in this we groan, earnestly desiring to be clothed with our habitation which is**

from heaven, 3 if indeed, having been clothed, we shall not be found naked. 4 For we who are in this tent groan, being burdened, not because we want to be unclothed, but further clothed, that mortality may be swallowed up by life. 5 Now He who has prepared us for this very thing is God, who also has given us the Spirit as a guarantee. 6 So we are always confident, knowing that while we are at home in the body we are absent from the Lord. 7 For we walk by faith, not by sight. 8 We are confident, yes, well pleased rather to be absent from the body and to be present with the Lord.

Paul knew his readers in the city of Corinth. Before believing in Jesus, they had been pagans who worshiped many gods. He is making the specific point that at death they will not be just bodiless spirits that have to pay to cross the dark river Styx.

In that day, when a Greek died his family put a coin in the corpse's mouth to pay the boatman. Otherwise they believed that their loved one wouldn't be allowed to cross into the land of the dead and would wander forever.

Instead, Paul says that, as believers in Jesus, whose sins have been forgiven, when we die there are glorious bodies awaiting us in the Heavenly Kingdom. Believe me, I'm looking forward to that. I looked a lot better about 45 years ago. But I'm going to look amazing 45 years from today.

However, the bodies that await us in Heaven right now are not our final glorified bodies. Those we will receive at the resurrection, when the graves are emptied.

There is a little cemetery in northern Oklahoma where the bodies of my mother, father and sister are waiting for that moment. As the Apostle Paul says, they are like seeds planted in the ground. Someday those bodies will rise to new life, but in the meantime my mother, father and sister are in Heaven.

But what about those who die and go to Hell? Do they lose their memories? Not according to Jesus. In Luke chapter 16 He tells the parable of Lazarus and the rich man. The rich man dies and goes to Hell. Clearly, he remembers everything about his former life and cares about his brothers who were still alive. The vividness of those memories increases his suffering. (Interestingly, this is the only parable in which Jesus uses the proper name of a person in the story.)

At the very beginning of his experience, Dr. Alexander's loss of personhood, loss of memory, of emotion and logic, with no sense of a body at all, fits far better with an Eastern mystical view of the afterlife than with anything that is Christian.

The ultimate goal of Eastern mystical Enlightenment is to advance the soul through Karma and Samsara to that place where it is no longer locked into the chaos of this physical realm and where the individual ceases to exist as an independent personality, instead losing all of self in the endless state of Nirvana.

From a Biblical perspective, Dr. Alexander's loss of personhood raises serious questions. The Bible is clear in the Book of Genesis that all humans have been given the Image of God. Certainly, that includes personality and personhood.

To have personhood, identity, and all logical faculties stripped away raises serious red flags regarding the nature of all that is to follow. Why would a loving God who created personhood and all our logical faculties do such a thing? In all of the Bible, whenever humans encounter God or His angels, this never happens. Not once. Not even in Hell.

Dr. Alexander writes that he became desperate to get out of the unpleasant place he calls the Earthworm's-Eye View. And get out he did. In the middle of the dark and dying biological ugliness that was all around him, something new appeared.

Chapter Six

Escaping the "womb" of death

Dr. Alexander's escape from the Earthworm's-Eye View was stunning. Here is how he described it: "Something new emerged from the darkness above: something that wasn't cold or dead or dark, but the exact opposite of all those things. If I tried for the rest of my life, I would never be able to do justice to this entity that now approached me...to come anywhere close to describing how beautiful it was." (page 32) "Turning slowly, it radiated fine filaments of white gold light and as it did so the darkness began to splinter apart." (page 38)

Dr. Alexander says that he began to hear what he calls "living sound, like the most complex beautiful piece of music..." And it grew, as pure white light descended upon him. It was a gateway of light and he was pulled upward through it with tremendous speed.

Immediately, he found himself in a completely new world that was the strangest and most stunningly beautiful that he had ever seen. To him, it felt like he was being born.

He found himself flying above a countryside that was green and lush. It was like earth, but it wasn't earth. He was passing over lovely trees and fields and waterways. Here and there he saw people, adults and children, laughing and playing. They sang and danced in circles. All of them wore simple, yet beautiful, clothes that were made of the same lovely warmth as the trees and flowers around them. (page 39)

He kept on flying – he didn't know for how long. At some point he realized that someone was flying next to him. It was a ravishingly lovely girl. They were riding along together on an intricately patterned surface filled with amazing colors which he described as "the wing of a butterfly."

The girl looked at him and in her look was love so wonderful that it made his whole life worth living just to get to that experience. Dr. Alexander describes it as a pure love that combined all other loves. Later he came to believe that this girl was a sister that he had lost in death years before.

Without using words, the girl "spoke" to him. Her message had three parts: First, she said, "You are loved and cherished dearly forever." Second, "You have nothing to fear." And third, "There is nothing you can do wrong." (Page 41) The girl told him that after he was shown many things he would go back. He didn't even know what back meant, because he had no memory or self-awareness at all.

In my opinion, this three-part message is the ultimate truth-claim of Dr. Alexander's entire experience. Everything else is presented to prove that this statement is true. He says that, just hearing it brought vast relief to him. Clearly, he believed that it related to his entire life. Notice that there are no qualifications about the girl's message. It is unconditional.

Also notice that it is not meant simply for Dr. Alexander, but for everyone who would read of his experience. He considers himself to be a messenger sent back with the ultimate consoling message about what happens when all of us die. That message is being accepted by millions of people right now. I understand that a film will be made of his book to spread the message even further.

Consequently, it is vital that we examine the truth-claims of the girl's statement. And our measuring rod will be the Bible, because the Bible presents itself as the ultimate authority about God, about man's true spiritual condition, about salvation and about Heaven.

First, the girl communicated, "You are loved and cherished dearly forever." This is a good beginning. **1 John 4:16** tells us this, **"We have known and believed the love that God has for us. God is love, and he who abides in love abides in God, and God in him."**

And we have the very familiar passage in **John 3:16-17** that says, **"For God so loved**

the world that He gave His only begotten Son, that whoever believes in Him should not perish but have everlasting life. For God did not send His Son into the world to condemn the world, but that the world through Him might be saved."

One of the greatest mistakes a person can make in studying the Bible is to cut out a text here or there, without any concern for the entire message of Scripture, and then use that text as the basis for all of his beliefs. This is called proof-texting and Satan, the Prince of Darkness, is the greatest proof-texter in the universe. He loves to cut and snip the Scripture to create half-truths.

Proof-texting from the Bible to present a half-truth is at the heart of so many cults and false religions. A half-truth was at the heart of the lie that Satan told Eve in the Garden of Eden. His greatest lies always include truth which he twists into his version of reality. Could that be what is about to happen here?

The second part of the girl's message was, "You have nothing to fear." Well, didn't Jesus say to His disciples, "Fear not?" Did He mean that for everyone through all of time?

It's true that we are loved dearly by God, but does that mean there is nothing to fear when we die? Clearly, in context, that is the meaning and import of the girl's statement. Unfortunately, what she said is in direct conflict with what Jesus Christ Himself said.

Over and over, He warned that we humans do, indeed, have a great deal to fear after death. Over and over, He warned about a place called Hell. According to Jesus, Hell is not an eternal party with an endless supply of booze. It is a place that should be desperately feared. According to Jesus, Hell is so real and so horrible that a person should be willing to take the most extreme measures to escape it. How strong was His warning?

Read His words in **Matthew 5:27-30**: **"You have heard that it was said to those of old, 'You shall not commit adultery.' 28 But I say to you that whoever looks at a woman to lust for her has already committed adultery with her in his heart. 29 If your right eye causes you to sin, pluck it out and cast it from you; for it is more profitable for you that one of your members perish, than for your whole body to be cast into hell. 30 And if your right** hand causes you to sin, cut it off and cast it from you; for it is more profitable for you that one of your members perish, than for your whole body to be cast into hell."

And in **Matthew 10:28** Jesus warns, **"Do not fear those who kill the body but cannot kill the soul. But rather fear Him who is able to destroy both soul and body in hell."** He is speaking about God Himself.

In **Mark 9:42-48** Jesus says, **"But whoever causes one of these little ones who believe in Me to stumble, it would be better for him if a millstone were hung around his neck, and he were thrown into the sea. 43 If your hand causes you to sin, cut it off. It is better for you to enter into life maimed, rather than having two hands, to go to hell, into the fire that shall never be quenched -- where 'Their worm does not die And the fire is not quenched.' 45 And if your foot causes you to sin, cut it off. It is better for you to enter life lame, rather than having two feet, to be cast into hell, into the fire that shall never be quenched -- 46 where 'Their worm does not die And the fire is not quenched.' 47 And if your eye causes you to sin, pluck it**

out. It is better for you to enter the kingdom of God with one eye, rather than having two eyes, to be cast into hell fire -- 48 where 'Their worm does not die And the fire is not quenched.'"

There could be no more serious warning about the afterlife. If we believe Jesus, there is much for all of us to fear. Most of all, we should fear God. That is what Jesus told us to do. How do we do it? We do it by taking sin seriously and not minimizing how deadly it is.

If a doctor told you that you have cancer, would you laugh it off? No, you would fear it. Because you feared it, you would do whatever you could to get healed. Jesus says that all of us have cancer of the soul. If that sin cancer isn't healed it will destroy us forever. How will our cancer be healed?

2 Peter 3:9 says, **The Lord is not slack concerning His promise, as some count slackness, but is longsuffering toward us, not willing that any should perish, but that all should come to repentance.**

Repentance for what? For the sin that is eating away at our lives and that will send us to Hell. Fear of that eternal death should lead to repentance for sin before God.

So one statement of truth, "God loves us dearly," is blended with a terrible lie, "We have nothing to fear." According to the Bible, the only people who have nothing to fear when they die are those who have been forgiven by God and who belong to Him. Everyone else should be desperately afraid enough to repent.

The first two parts of the girl's statement culminate in the ultimate falsehood, a desperate lie designed to make us believe that repentance for sin is not necessary. She says to Dr. Alexander, "You can do no wrong."

If those words are true, the entire Bible is nothing but a lie, because from beginning to end it tells us that, not only do we *do* wrong, we *are* wrong at the core of our souls. The cancer of sin is systemic and terminal. But then the Bible shows how God has made a way to save us and make us fit for the real Heaven.

First, there was the sacrificial system in the Old Testament showing how serious sin really is and how a blood price, the price of a life, must be paid for it. This culminated in the New Testament with Jesus, the Son of God, who came to be our Substitute, who gave His life to pay the price for our sin and make us right and clean and pure before a Holy and Just God.

So, according to the Bible, Dr. Alexander has been told a lie beyond all lies. To make certain that he believes it and will communicate it to the world, he is taken deeper into an amazing and confirming vision. Here are his words:

"I was in a place of clouds...big puffy pink-white ones that showed up sharply against a deep blue-black sky." (One is tempted to say that this comes perilously close to what might be called a "culturally expected" vision.) "Higher than the clouds - immeasurably higher - were flocks of transparent orbs, shimmering beings arced across the sky, leaving streamer-like lines behind them.

"Birds? Angels? ...neither of these words do justice to the beings themselves which were quite simply different from anything I have known on this planet. They were more advanced. Higher. A sound huge and booming like a glorious chant came down from above..." (Page 45)

Later Dr. Alexander felt that it was pure joy coming from these creatures. He could hear the visual beauty of the silvery bodies of these beings and see the surging, joyful perfection of what they sang.

In <u>Proof of Heaven</u>, Dr. Alexander says much more about the beauty of all that he saw and how it transformed his understanding of reality. But I want to focus on a particular passage that is of tremendous importance.

Chapter Seven

Welcome to the Core

Dr. Alexander's journey took him into an amazing *presence*:

"I continued moving forward and found myself entering an immense void, completely dark, infinite in size, yet also infinitely comforting. Pitch black as it was, it was also brimming over with light, a light that seemed to come from a brilliant orb that I sensed near me."

Dr. Alexander believed that he was in the Presence of God, the Creator. He continues: "This being was so close that there didn't seem to be any distance between God and myself. Yet, at the same time I could sense the infinite vastness of the Creator, could see how completely minuscule I was by comparison.

"I will occasionally use Om as the pronoun for God...Om was the sound I remembered hearing associated with that omniscient, omnipotent and unconditionally loving God..." (page 47) Dr. Alexander felt that the orb was there as a kind of companion interpreter between himself and God.

It's important to point out that "Om" is a mystical and sacred syllable used as an incantation associated with the Hindu gods Brahma, Vishnu and Shiva. It is referred to as omkara and is intoned as a name of God in both Hinduism and Buddhism. As such, it is an invitation to those gods to come and partake in sacrifices.

But does any of that matter? Isn't one name for God as good as another?

One of the greatest mistakes that the Children of Israel made when they entered the Promised Land of Canaan was to integrate their system of worship with that of the pagan cultures around them. This didn't happen overnight. It happened subtly and one of the keys to it was the renaming of God.

What did the God of the Bible tell Moses to call Him? **Exodus 3:13-14** says this: **Then Moses said to God, "Indeed, when I come to the children of Israel and say to them, 'The God of your fathers has sent me to you,' and they say to me, 'What is His name?' what shall I say to them?" And God said to Moses, "I AM WHO I AM." And He said, "Thus you shall say to the children of Israel, 'I AM has sent me to you.'"**

This is known as the Tetragrammaton. From Hebrew, it is translated YHWH, from which we get Yahweh/Jehovah. Ancient Hebrew had no vowels, so translators added them to make the Name of God pronounceable.

When the Israelites entered Canaan they confronted many other gods. One of the chief deities of the land was known as Baal. Now "baal" is an interchangeable word. It can mean just a human lord or ruler, a title denoting respect. But, also, it was the name of a specific pagan sky deity that was thought to copulate with a female earth deity known as

Astarte or Ashtoreth to produce each year's crops.

I'm sure it was easy for the Israelites to start calling Yahweh, baal. After all, wasn't it just a title that meant lord? But false naming became part of the seduction that took them into the vileness and murder of pagan worship and destroyed their relationship with the One True God. Ultimately, it brought terrible judgment upon them.

This marriage of pagan theology and worship with Biblical theology and worship is called syncretism. And renaming is always part of it. Perhaps the greatest mistake that Roman Catholicism has made from the time of Constantine onward has been syncretism, the blending of Christianity with paganism in a misguided attempt to make the faith easier to understand and accept. At the center of it is renaming. Pagan deities were renamed with the names of angels, apostles, martyrs and saints.

This renaming goes on today even among evangelical Christians. There are people who believe that "Allah" is just a name for God and Christians who want to be understood by Muslims should use it. In my opinion, that is a grave error.

Not only is there a pagan name for God in Dr. Alexander's vision, he is given an "orb" to be the interpreter who speaks for this God. (An interesting side note: Many who have UFO experiences describe what they saw as orbs.)

What might the Bible have to say about this "companion interpreter" who reveals "God" to Dr. Alexander? **1 Timothy 2:5** is clear, **"For there is one God and one Mediator between God and men, the Man Christ Jesus."**

What is a mediator? A mediator is one who goes between two parties. A vital key to good mediation is accurately transferring information between those parties. But in the context of this verse the meaning of the word is much broader and deeper.

Because Jesus was the Mediator who paid the price for our sin, taking our penalty on Himself before a Just and Holy God, He is the revealer of all truth about God. As the Mediator, Jesus is the only reliable interpreter of God, because He has an absolutely unique relationship with Him. According to **John**

14:11, Jesus and the Father are One. He told His disciples that, when they saw Him, they were seeing the Father.

After His resurrection, Jesus entered into an absolutely unique position of authority in His relationship to God. **Hebrews 1:1-13** tells us this:

"God, who at various times and in various ways spoke in time past to the fathers by the prophets, 2 has in these last days spoken to us by His Son, whom He has appointed heir of all things, through whom also He made the worlds; 3 who being the brightness of His glory and the express image of His person, and upholding all things by the word of His power, when He had by Himself purged our sins, sat down at the right hand of the Majesty on high, 4 having become so much better than the angels, as He has by inheritance obtained a more excellent name than they.

5 For to which of the angels did He ever say: "You are My Son, today I have begotten You"? And again: "I will be to Him a Father, and He shall be to Me a Son"? 6 But when He again brings the firstborn into the world, He says: "Let all the angels

of God worship Him." 7 And of the angels He says: "Who makes His angels spirits and His ministers a flame of fire." 8 But to the Son He says: "Your throne, O God, is forever and ever; a scepter of righteousness is the scepter of Your kingdom. 9 You have loved righteousness and hated lawlessness; therefore God, Your God, has anointed You with the oil of gladness more than Your companions." 10 And: "You, LORD, in the beginning laid the foundation of the earth, and the heavens are the work of Your hands. 11 They will perish, but You remain; and they will all grow old like a garment; 12 Like a cloak You will fold them up, and they will be changed. But You are the same, and Your years will not fail."

13 But to which of the angels has He ever said: "Sit at My right hand, till I make Your enemies Your footstool"?

An interpreter reveals. The purpose for the orb that Dr. Alexander saw was to reveal this "God" to him. Yet Jesus said this in **Matthew 11:27**: **"All things have been delivered to Me by My Father, and no one knows the Son except the Father. Nor does**

anyone know the Father except the Son, and *the one to whom the Son wills to reveal Him.* So no one is going to have God revealed to him unless Jesus wills it. Why is Jesus in a unique position to reveal God? Because He **is** God.

One thing is very clear. Jesus is not Dr. Alexander's "God." Never would Jesus call Himself "Om" or the name of any other pagan deity. Neither is He the "orb interpreter" for "Om." Throughout the history of Christianity, when Jesus appears to an individual, that person knows it is Jesus (at least eventually, if not at first). And Jesus is not present anywhere in Dr. Alexander's vision.

Yet, Dr. Alexander is very concerned that we not think of Om as distant or impersonal. He is, after all, speaking to a western culture that is both self-centered and still influenced to some degree by the personal God of the Bible. While he never mentions Jesus, he says this:

"But - again paradoxically - Om is "human" as well – even more human than you and I are. Om understands and sympathizes with our human situation more profoundly and personally than we can ever imagine because Om knows what we have forgotten, and understands the terrible burden it is to live with amnesia of the divine for even a moment." (page 86)

In what sense is "Om" "human?" Did he become a man and live among us, dying for our sins? If he had, I'm sure he would have mentioned it. But in "Om's" theological universe such a sacrifice is not necessary. Our problem isn't sin. Our problem is *bad memory*, which we will discover in a moment.

All of this leads to one inescapable conclusion. The "god" revealed in <u>Proof of Heaven</u> is not the God of the Bible. Such a conclusion becomes even more certain as we read more of what "Om" communicates to Dr. Alexander.

Chapter Eight

The message from "Om"

"Through the Orb, Om told me that there is not one universe, but many...but that love lay at the center of them all. Evil was present in all the other universes as well, but only in the tiniest trace amounts. Evil was necessary because without it freewill was impossible, and without freewill there could be no growth – no forward movement, no chance for us to become what God longed for us to be." (Page 48)

This is both fascinating and deeply disturbing. It is just another form of the lie that Satan told Eve in the Garden of Eden.

In essence the serpent in the Garden said, "Evil is needed. If you eat of the fruit you will know both good and evil. That's the only way to be wise and being wise is good. It's spiritual growth. You can't really know what good is unless you know what evil is. You can't really be like a god yourself without knowing both." According to Satan, knowing evil is half the key to spiritual ascendance.

So here is the inescapable logic of "Om's" statement: If what he said is true then God is the creator of evil. He must be because, according to his statement, evil is necessary for freewill to exist. If God has created freewill and if freewill is necessary for spiritual growth, and if evil is necessary to have freewill, then God must have created evil, because like good, evil is essential to the eternal creative and transformative purpose.

In this construct, where would evil have come from if not from God? This leads to a terrifying conclusion: God must have evil *in him* which he externalizes into the universe for all of us to enjoy. Of course, in very "tiny trace amounts."

How would this philosophy of evil that came from Dr. Alexander's Core "God" apply to practical human life and experience? Let's say that you are a woman and you marry a man. Just by establishing that marriage relationship you have created a new set of possible choices for your husband. Those choices did not exist before the marriage relationship was established. Either he can treat you with love and kindness or he can beat the living hell out of you and be unfaithful to you.

If he chooses the latter did you create the evil that he chose? Was the existence of that evil *necessary* for him to choose to love and cherish you in order for the relationship to grow? Did evil have to be there? It did according to "Om."

Let's be honest, to think this way is insane. More than that, it is satanic. There are evil people in this world who blame abused women for the horrible things that are done to them. The heart of that hellish logic, the necessity of evil for freewill to exist, is right here in the Core of Dr. Alexander's heaven. It is the heart of his "God." No matter how sugarcoated and beautiful it looks, it is infinitely filthier than good old healthy feces.

The view of the Bible about freewill is exactly the opposite. Freewill existed before evil and does not depend upon it. In the Book of Genesis, before the Fall of Adam and Eve into sin, it says that Adam named the animals that were brought before him. Clearly, this was an expression of free choice and free will and the presence of evil was not necessary for him to carry out the task.

Laughably, "Om" informs Dr. Alexander that only a "tiny trace" of evil is necessary in all the universes of God's creation. I assume he includes ours in the lot. Aren't we thankful that no more than a trace was needed here? Hmm, where did all the rest come from?

Imagine this: You have a cold clear glass of mountain spring water in your hand. It's totally pure and safe to drink. How much feces in the glass would be necessary to keep you from drinking it? A heaping spoonful?

You wouldn't drink it if you knew that there was a microscopic drop in it, would you? A microscopic drop might not kill you, but it would pollute the whole thing. No longer would you consider that water to be pure. And microscopic drops of filth have a disturbing tendency to grow, don't they?

And so it is with evil in any universe. The tiniest trace pollutes the whole. This argument that "just a trace of evil is necessary and, by implication, is acceptable" would be insanely hilarious if it were not so lethally tragic.

Would Dr. Alexander use this logic in his medical practice? Would he allow just a few microbes of MRSA, a resistant staph infection, into a patient's brain during surgery? Would he say, "Why worry about it? It's just a tiny trace."

I'm sure, as a caring medical professional, he would be desperate to destroy a single microbe of that hellish infection. If he knew it was present, he wouldn't begin the surgery. In his own case, it was just a tiny trace of E. Coli that almost killed him. Yet, he willingly accepts "trace amounts of evil" as needed for freewill to exist. In the Garden of Eden there was just a tiny trace of evil and it has been killing us ever since.

This message from "Om" is Ultimate Darkness from Hell and a justification for Satan and all his evil works. Indeed, Dr. Alexander saw a great Darkness in this being he believed was "God." He calls it "the vast inky black core that was the home of the divine itself." (page 48)

How does Dr. Alexander's inky black core "God," compare with the God of the Bible: **1 John 1:5-7** says: **"This is the message which we have heard from Him and declare to you, that God is light and in Him is no darkness at all. 6 If we say that we have fellowship with Him, and walk in darkness, we lie and do not practice the truth. 7 But if we walk in the light as He is in the light, we have fellowship with one another, and the blood of Jesus Christ His Son cleanses us from all sin.**

So where does evil really come from? The Book of James is clear about that. **James 1:12-15** says **"Blessed is the man who endures temptation; for when he has been approved, he will receive the crown of life which the Lord has promised to those who love Him. 13 Let no one say when he is tempted, "I am tempted by God"; for God**

cannot be tempted by evil, nor does He Himself tempt anyone. 14 But each one is tempted when he is drawn away by his own desires and enticed. 15 Then, when desire has conceived, it gives birth to sin; and sin, when it is full-grown, brings forth death.

Logically, if God created even the tiniest trace of evil because it was necessary for freewill, then He created temptation, because the two are inextricably linked. But according to James, temptation comes when we allow wrong desires to control us. It comes from the abuse of the freewill that God has given to us. God has created us to be free moral agents. We are free to desire wrong things and act upon those desires. But just like the choice to be unfaithful to your marriage partner, all forms of sin are *our* responsibility, not God's.

However, the Bible teaches that there is a Cosmic Evil that is beyond this world and deeply influences the evil choices and actions in human life. Jesus Himself pointed to the source of it. In **John 8:44-45** He said this to people who were accusing Him of being evil:

"**You are of your father the devil, and the desires of your father you want to do. He was a murderer from the beginning, and does not stand in the truth, because there is no truth in him. When he speaks a lie, he speaks from his own resources, for he is a liar and the father of it.**"

In **Matthew 4:3** Satan is called the "Tempter." A tempter is someone who attempts to manipulate freewill in order to entice or persuade an individual to do wrong and to believe wrong. Temptation is always toward something desirable.

Chapter Nine

Can we be separated from God?

As <u>Proof of Heaven</u> continues, Dr. Alexander communicates more and more of the great lie that Satan has been promulgating through all of time:

"Now, however, I knew that I was part of the divine and that nothing – absolutely nothing – could ever take that away. The (false) suspicion that we could somehow be separated from God is the root of every form of anxiety in the universe and the cure for it - which I received partially in the Gateway and completely from the Core was the knowledge that nothing can tear us from God ever. This knowledge...remains the single most important thing I've ever learned..." (page 76)

Here are a few other excerpts of wisdom that he received from the Core: "Freewill is of central importance for our function in the earthly realm: a function that, we will all one day discover, serves the much higher role of our ascendance in the timeless alternate dimension...our role here is to grow toward the divine. And that growth is closely watched by the beings in the world above – the souls and the lucent orbs..." (page 84)

"Our truest deepest self is completely free. It is not crippled or compromised by past actions or concerned with identity or status. It comprehends that it has no need to fear the earthly world and therefore, it has no need to build itself up through fame and wealth or conquest.

"This is the true spiritual self that all of us are destined someday to recover. But until that day comes, I feel, we should do everything in our power to get in touch with this miraculous aspect of ourselves – to cultivate it and bring it to light. This is the being living within all of us right now and that is, in fact, the being that God truly intends us to be. How do we get closer to this genuine spiritual self? By manifesting love and compassion." (page 85)

So according to Om, growing toward the "divine" that is in all of us, simply means manifesting love and compassion? What is the Bible's response:

Romans 3:23 is desperately clear in its disagreement: **"For all have sinned and fall short of the glory of God. And Rom 6:23 For the wages of sin is death, but the gift of God is eternal life in Christ Jesus our Lord."**

Once again, the message of the Bible is exactly the opposite of the one Dr. Alexander received. Our sin has separated us from God. Unless God does a miracle and saves us by His grace and power, we will fall short forever. We can never "grow into divinity." The power is not in us.

The Bible puts it this way in **Isaiah 64:6-7**: **"But we are all like an unclean thing, and all our righteousnesses are like filthy rags; we all fade as a leaf, and our iniquities, like the wind, have taken us away.   And there is no one who calls on**

Your name, who stirs himself up to take hold of You; for You have hidden Your face from us, and have consumed us because of our iniquities."

Thank God He did make a way in Jesus for us to be cleansed from unrighteousness and escape the eternal enslavement and penalty of sin. But to find God's way we've got to stop believing the lie that we are "little divinities" with nothing more wrong with us than a bad case of amnesia. Doesn't that strike you as ridiculous? Doesn't it feel just a little too self-serving and convenient? As you look at the desperate condition of humanity in the world, does the message from "Om" feel like the answer?

So how do we find God's true way of Salvation?

During his message to the Greeks in Athens, the Apostle Paul said these words: **Acts 17:29-31 "Since we are the offspring of God, we ought not to think that the Divine Nature is like gold or silver or stone, something shaped by art and man's devising. 30 Truly, these times of ignorance God overlooked, but now commands all men everywhere to repent,**

31 because He has appointed a day on which He will judge the world in righteousness by the Man whom He has ordained. He has given assurance of this to all by raising Him from the dead."

So the Divine Nature is not something that can be shaped by "art or man's devising." In ancient times this meant creating images of the gods out of physical materials to worship. Also it meant that you couldn't shape a divine nature in yourself through esoteric philosophy and the mystery religions.

In our day it means that we can't mold the Image of God in ourselves by our own efforts because we think we are little gods rediscovering our divinity. Certainly this includes trying to reconstruct my "godhood" through acts of love and compassion, as important as acts of love and compassion truly are. All of these methods are different forms of ignorance. What does God require? Repentance for sin. And when we face that it leads us straight to Jesus.

According to the New Testament, Jesus is the center of everything. **Acts 4:12** says, **"Nor is there salvation in any other, for**

there is no other name under heaven given among men by which we must be saved."

With all of its scintillating beauty, at the heart of Dr. Alexander's vision there is darkness and tragedy, because the most beautiful person in Heaven is Jesus and He is totally absent from this "proof" of "Heaven."

Nowhere in the vision is there the truth about sin and the need for repentance and salvation through the blood of God's Son that was shed for us. Jesus is mentioned only briefly when Dr. Alexander visits a church after his ordeal. To him, a painting of Jesus breaking bread with his disciples evokes his "communion with the Core."

While Dr. Alexander was in a coma there were people praying for him, including a channeler who believed that she contacted him psychically. After a week in which he was brain dead, and when his family was about to pull the plug, he came back to consciousness with no brain damage. A true miracle.

To his credit, Dr. Alexander does his best in Proof of Heaven to counter the arguments and criticisms from secular materialist scientists such as he was. As expected, his counter arguments have had little effect on those committed to a materialist world view.

Chapter Ten

What did Dr. Alexander really experience?

First, as beautiful and wonderful as it was, based on the Bible it was not the Heaven of God, because in the Heaven of God, Jesus is King. He is the center. He is on the throne. No one can enter Heaven without going through Him. This is absolutely clear in **John 14:6 Jesus said to him, "I am the way, the truth, and the life. No one comes to the Father except through Me.**

So what are we to make of Dr. Alexander's experience? It should be a cautionary tale for all who are followers of Jesus.

In **2 Corinthians 11:13-15** the Apostle Paul warns against false teachers. In that passage he says this: **"For such are false apostles, deceitful workers, transforming themselves into apostles of Christ. 14 And no wonder! For Satan himself transforms himself into an angel of light. 15 Therefore it is no great thing if his ministers also transform themselves into ministers of righteousness, whose end will be according to their works."**

Satan can transform himself into an angel of light. What does angelic light mean? It means the personification of glory, wisdom, and power, the godlike appearance of ravishing, ultimate reality. In the Bible, when angels appeared to people the automatic response was a desire to worship them.

What did Dr. Alexander really experience? Satan is the greatest illusionist who has ever lived. From the perspective of the Bible, the vision in <u>Proof of Heaven</u> is nothing less than an amazing, breathtaking delusion of ecstasy, created to make him into an unwitting, yet totally willing, messenger carrying the ultimate lie.

What should we take away from Dr. Alexander's experience? That this being whom we call Satan and who was once called Lucifer, Son of the Morning, known among his followers as the Light Bearer, is powerful beyond our ability to imagine. He is able to create an appearance and experience of love, majesty and heavenly wonder that is so scintillatingly beautiful and so apparently real that an honest, ethical brilliant scientist and medical doctor would be utterly fooled by it. And millions are believing that vision.

While there have been many such delusions over the centuries, the one given to Dr. Alexander comes with a specificity and authority that is rare. Also it comes at a cataclysmic period of history.

In **2 Thessalonians 2:7-12** the Apostle Paul writes some very sobering words: **For the mystery of lawlessness is already at work; only He who now restrains will do so until He is taken out of the way. 8 And then the lawless one will be revealed, whom the Lord will consume with the**

breath of His mouth and destroy with the brightness of His coming. 9 The coming of the lawless one is according to the working of Satan, with all power, signs, and lying wonders, 10 and with all unrighteous deception among those who perish, because they did not receive the love of the truth, that they might be saved. 11 And for this reason God will send them strong delusion, that they should believe the lie, 12 that they all may be condemned who did not believe the truth but had pleasure in unrighteousness.

The Greatest Lie, the most fantastic Illusion and Delusion that has ever existed is coming to this world. Just like the beautiful lie that Dr. Alexander experienced it will appear to be eternally real and all-encompassing. The Core of that delusion will present a "God" not found in the Bible. Unless you know the Word of God and are filled with the Spirit of Jesus, you will not be able to stand against it. The outlines of that Greatest Lie are becoming clearer every day.

Chapter Eleven

What questions should he have asked?

In <u>Proof of Heaven</u>, Dr. Alexander reports that, over and over, during his wonderful vision he asked, "What is this? Where is this place? Is this Heaven?" Apparently, he never got an answer. Instead, he was shown ever-increasing loveliness and ecstasy. He asked the wrong questions.

If Dr. Alexander had known and believed the Bible he would have asked a different question. He would have asked, "Who is Jesus?" The answer to that (or lack of an answer) would have clarified everything.

In **1 Corinthians 12:3** the Apostle Paul tells us this: **"Therefore I make known to you that no one speaking by the Spirit of God calls Jesus accursed, and no one can say that Jesus is Lord except by the Holy Spirit."**

This is the great test. I have read accounts of many visions, out of body experiences (OBE's) and near death experiences (NDE's). Beautiful creatures of light who are really servants of darkness will say many nice things about Jesus. They will call him Teacher, Prophet and Avatar and much more, but never will they say, "Jesus is Lord," because He is not their Lord.

There is another question that must be asked. **1 John 4:1-6** says, **"Beloved, do not believe every spirit, but test the spirits, whether they are of God; because many false prophets have gone out into the world. 2 By this you know the Spirit of God: Every spirit that confesses that Jesus Christ has come in the flesh is of God, 3 and every spirit that does not confess that**

Jesus Christ has come in the flesh is not of God. And this is the spirit of the Antichrist, which you have heard was coming, and is now already in the world.

4 You are of God, little children, and have overcome them, because He who is in you is greater than he who is in the world. 5 They are of the world. Therefore they speak as of the world, and the world hears them. 6 We are of God. He who knows God hears us; he who is not of God does not hear us. By this we know the spirit of truth and the spirit of error.

John presents a simple, but vital test to determine the true origin of the most beautiful angel, orb or entity that might present itself to us: Did Jesus the Messiah, the Christ, the Son of God, actually come in the flesh? This means was He really born of a woman? Did He enter the world as a baby and grow up to be a man? The Powers of Darkness are happy to say that He was a Great Prophet. They will say that the "Christ Consciousness" came upon the man Jesus at His baptism and left Him before He died on the cross.

This is one of the major tenets of Gnosticism, an ancient philosophy that attempts to syncretize Christianity with Eastern metaphysical thought. But the Powers of Darkness will never say that God Himself was born of a woman, took on a human body and became a man. This act brings the Glory of the Godhead straight into the human race.

Why do they refuse to admit that such a wonderful thing ever happened? Because beneath the glowing façade of exquisite lies and the promise of power, Satan and his Lords of Darkness despise the physical world. They despise the fact that the Eternal God put His Image into human creatures made of flesh and confirmed His Love for us by becoming One of us.

I have spent decades studying the occult, esoteric philosophies and the purposes and personifications of supernatural Evil. Here is what I have come to believe:

Satan and his Lords of Darkness view humans the way we view cattle. They attempt to fatten us on the corn of their intricate and lovely prevarications because they consider our souls to be their food. Like vampires (from which that mythology grew), they draw strength from our fears and addictions, our hates and agonies. Most of all, they gain their greatest pleasure when we grow angry with God and turn away from believing in Him, when we become what they want us to be – our own little idol makers worshipping ourselves.

These beings despise God because of what He has done for us. They despise Jesus, God's Son, because He defeated them on the Cross. They know His deep love for humanity, His overwhelming desire that we repent and come back to Him. In the depth of their hate, there is only one way that they can bring pain to the Eternal One and that is by hurting us and doing what they can to help separate us from His Love.

In the years ahead I believe that we will see more near death visions such as the one given to Dr. Alexander. They can be very confusing. In many of them Jesus Himself will seem to appear. Though He was not present in Dr. Alexander's vision, He has seemed to appear in many others. What are we to make of this?

In 1972 a book was published entitled
<u>Seth Speaks: The Eternal Validity of the Soul</u>.
(© 1972 by Jane Roberts, Prentice-Hall) It purports to be
the work of an "entity" called Seth who is "no
longer focused in physical reality. It is
claimed that the book was "channeled" by this
"entity" through the body of a woman named
Jane Roberts. "Seth" has much to say about
the human condition. Needless to say, it does
not agree with the Bible.

He informs us that a vast charade is
often enacted at death in which spirit "guides"
take on the form of the prophet or the deity
that the individual imagines that he believes
in. If it is Mohammed, then the spirit appears
as Mohammed, if Krishna, then Krishna, if
Jesus, then Jesus, etc.

According to Seth, all of this is for the
purpose of "helping" the newly dead
individual to get beyond these
"hallucinations." He claims that the way the
spirits do this is by gaining the person's trust.
According to Seth this is why they appear as
Jesus or Moses, etc.

Apart from his seemingly endless
blather (Seth has an exalted view of his
intellectual and literary gifts), it may be that

he has inadvertently revealed something important. During NDE's, false spirits can make themselves look like Jesus. (I was first introduced to this idea and the glories of Seth in a book entitled Life, Death and Beyond by J. Kerby Anderson © 1980 Zondervan Corporation. I recommend it.)

Jesus predicted in Matthew 24 that, before His second coming, many false Christs would appear in this world spreading all kinds of lies. Would it not be predictable that they would take the opportunity to mislead people when they were on the threshold of death in order to send back their lying messages?

So if one appears to be Jesus, another test is in order. What message does this "Jesus" give to the individual to take back to the world? If it does not agree in *every part* with the Bible it is not from the real Jesus, no matter how wonderful and how loving the spirit and the experience appear to be.

Most often, a false message from a pseudo-Jesus will tell that we humans are destroying the environment and are about to destroy ourselves through war and nuclear holocaust. It will tell us that we need to love each other and grow toward divinity, etc. Once again, half truths coupled with lies. Never will a pseudo-Jesus talk about sin and the need for redemption. (Incidentally, it is reported that these same messages are given to UFO "abductees.")

Chapter Twelve

Which will you believe?

As I wrote at the beginning, the crisis issue for the entire human race is authority. What authority will you choose to guide your life? In the case presented in <u>Proof of Heaven</u>, the issue is clear. As honest as he is, and as much as I respect Dr. Alexander for the wonderful medical work he has done, we cannot accept the authority of his vision and, at the same time, accept the clear statements of the Bible. So which will you choose? What you choose will matter forever.

If you do not know Jesus, the Messiah, I urge you to place your faith in Him. Believe that He died and rose again to pay the price for your sins and pray to Him right now. Ask Him to forgive your sins and give you a new life, one that will last forever in God's true Heaven. Give your heart to him. Tell Him that you want Him to be your Lord and Master and to guide you every day. If you are doing this, please write to me through my website: www.colemanluck.com. I'd love to hear from you.

If you are a Christian, I urge you to buy Dr. Alexander's book and read it. Pray for him that God would open his eyes. Also, pray for the millions he is leading into the eternal darkness and everlasting sorrow of a false god.

Coleman Luck is a Hollywood writer and executive producer known for such TV series as "The Equalizer" and "Gabriel's Fire." He is a mentalist and a member of the Academy of Magical Arts at The Magic Castle in Hollywood. His first novel, <u>Angel Fall</u>, was published in 2009 by Zondervan, a subsidiary of Harper/Collins. His second novel, <u>The Mentalist Prophecies - Book One – Dagon's Illusion,</u> was published in 2013.

Coleman studied the Bible at the Moody Bible Institute in Chicago where his father, the late Dr. G. Coleman Luck, Sr. was a professor and chairman of the Bible department. Coleman received his undergraduate degree from Northern Illinois University (magna cum laude) and did graduate study at both the University of Southern California and Simon Greenleaf School of Law where he studied under noted cults expert, Dr. Walter Martin.

Coleman is a former U. S. Army infantry officer and decorated combat veteran with two bronze stars from Vietnam. He and his wife of 46 years, Carel Gage Luck, a fine artist, live in the mountains of central California.

Visit his website: www.colemanluck.com

Printed in Great Britain
by Amazon.co.uk, Ltd.,
Marston Gate.